G000136818

Sailing from Polruan

by
Tim Stapleton

Grosvenor House
Publishing Limited

Pont Pill, The Gribbin, St Austell Bay, Dodman

This book is published by
Grosvenor House Publishing Ltd
Link House
140 The Broadway, Tolworth, Surrey, KT6 7HT.
www.grosvenorhousepublishing.co.uk

A CIP record for this book
is available from the British Library

ISBN 978-1-83975-031-1

INTRODUCTION

I first came across Polruan in 1960 when it took me one and a half hours to walk the road from Polperro, where my parents had a cottage, to Polruan to cross on the passenger ferry, to Town Quay, to what is now the Gallants dinghy park, to hire a boat for the day. After that it was sailing, where sailing could be found, a first cruise from Sussex to the Channel Isles, the Norfolk Broads and a much travelled Enterprise dinghy (blue sails) in Polperro, London Reservoirs, Christchurch and with the children in Bristol docks.

In the 1970s we rented cottages in Polruan and in the 1980s I regularly crewed for Tony Edwards in Ondina of Polruan where we visited all points east and west. In the 1990s I sailed our much loved Drascombe Lugger and for the last 20 years a Crabber 17, now reclassified as a Shrimper, both with red sails and traditional lines.

The defining feature of Polruan is its inaccessibility, which is its strength and perhaps its weakness. This now shapes what happens throughout the seasons in the tourism economy. During my 60 years of knowledge, the proportion of young people going to university has increased tenfold from 5% to 50%. In the last 100 years the white van man has replaced the trading schooner whose construction and wares created the 40 shops that are no more in Polruan. These two factors alone for which no one is to blame, created the new Polruan holiday economy, based on a 100 letting cottages; nothing is forever. Of course since the arrival of the railways and the construction of the Fowey Hotel and villas in the 1880s, Fowey on the other side of the Estuary, has been a destination for holidays.

Within the harbour and river there are 1,500 moorings for leisure craft, almost all yachts and the necessary supporting facilities: Clubs, boatyards, storage, engineers and chandlers. Toms Boatyard has been developed so that the reinforced slip and boatlift can handle boats of up to 200 tonnes and typically five are undergoing work at any one time.

Despite the China Clay business slowing, we still see 10,000 tonne ships being skillfully turned in the river by tugs and towed to the docks. Large cruise ships arrive in the early morning and leave that evening, during eight months of the year. The harbour, equidistant between Plymouth and Falmouth, receives over 6,000 yachts a year, each of which support the leisure and tourism economy. The harbour, more intimate than its half dozen larger neighbours in the South West, has offered me much as a home port. I hope I have captured that experience and the elusive magic of sailing.

CONTENTS

1. REGATTA WEEK

Local regattas were very much a feature of the late nineteenth century with both sailing and rowing. Each harbour had its own class but as time went on handicaps were needed for visiting yachts. The whole was enlivened by brass bands, traders joined in, competitions and traditions quickly developed.

Dressed For Regatta Week 1999. Polruan Pontoon

In the 1920s the wealthy big yacht sailing enthusiasts got things organised. They would come down with their families to the summer villas in South Devon and Cornwall. Crews of twenty plus were needed to sail their yachts down to Falmouth and then spend consecutive weeks racing in Falmouth, Fowey and Dartmouth. The crews then sailed back to the Solent and the owners went back to work in the City in September. Thankfully they now continue to spend their money on super yachts, built in Falmouth, Plymouth and the Solent.

Big yacht regattas reached their peak in the 1930s with the giant J Class. There are some good records and mementos of their sailing in Fowey including Velsheda, still racing in the Solent. In the 1990s I attended one of the Winter talks at the Royal Fowey Yacht Club (RFYC) where an elderly retired MP Sir Reginald Bennett entertained us with his account as a young crew in the 1930s listening to Sir Arthur Quiller Couch, Commodore from 1911 – 1944 giving instructions at the start of Regatta Week. Much has changed and yet much has stayed the same. We still enjoy a hint of the 1930s on Monday afternoon with the Falmouth flotilla joining our cruisers racing back after Sunday. The Navy has been too stretched for the last 20 years for a passing frigate to be moored where a cruise liner is now more likely.

St Austell Bay offers great opportunities to set courses for the cruisers. A triangular course for the rest with some variation for the Falmouth Working Boats can be easily watched from the Polruan cliffs. Communications and fast safety boats have done much to manage the racing but we are all servants of the wind. We oscillate between the occasional 'racing cancelled for the day' when only the bar profits, and no wind until 10am and dinghys all need a tow out, particularly if the tide is coming in. I once managed to collect a tow of five Fowey Rivers. Then a delayed start as the Race Officer tries to position the starting buoy to set a good long beat to the first buoy and decided how many laps; easy to shorten, impossible to lengthen.

Old friends meet up and are surprised that another year has gone by but there are changes: a few less cruisers each year as committed crews are less available; a renaissance in Fowey Rivers whose colourful sails dominate the triangular course; family boats with local owners, often sailed by their children on holiday; the Troys, holding their own, with a crew of three, competitive to the last, sailed with cunning as to the right course and when to fly the spinnaker; fast small single handers and the smaller classes falling away. Not a single Mirror to be seen, plywood all rotted away, in which so many of us learnt to sail during our childhood.

There is much more to Regatta Week than the sailing; the social side of parties and music; the Carnival on Wednesday, competitions from crabbing to swimming and the pilot gigs at the end of the week. Beneath the surface and in all regattas are the unsung volunteers ashore and afloat who make it all happen, based on years of experience, so that you hardly notice them, though more are always needed.

Traditions grow rapidly, sailors doubting the accuracy of the handicaps, race marks which disappear in the mist. One of the more surprising, particularly for visitors, occurs on Wednesday afternoon. The Fowey Harbour Commissioner's (FHC) mooring barge manned by the Town 'Band', badly named, is moored on Polruan Quay. The Band adjourn to the pubs and the Giant Pasty, until fifteen years ago, cooked by the Polruan baker, is collected. After several hours with most of the band back on board, this 'sails' from Polruan for Town Quay, illuminated by red distress flares and smoke to feed the hungry children of Fowey. Yet we are always told 'Fowey is the money side and Polruan is the sunny side', one of those is still true.

Collecting the Giant Pasty, Polruan Quay

In conclusion, Fowey Harbour continues to flourish as a marina free zone, which encourages a sailors' harbour. One day the China Clay business will decline to the extent that the docks are not viable and the docks and access road will provide the essential infrastructure. By then I hope the regulatory framework will be sufficiently powerful to overwhelm the commercial case, which will be strong.

2. FALMOUTH WORKING BOATS

With, or more recently, without The Red Arrows and their display, which was often shortened by cloud at 6pm, the highlight of the Regatta on the Thursday is the Falmouth Working Boats race inside the harbour. They race up from Falmouth on the Monday with the returning Fowey cruiser fleet and moor up on the pontoon opposite Town Quay. The Class continues to thrive through the retention of traditional fishing techniques, dredging for oysters under sail. As a result the oyster beds are sustainable and the boat preserved, supporting the skills of local boatyards. During the week, in light airs, they are dependant on launches to tow them to the start line, a mile or so offshore. In celebration of their 70th anniversary visit in 2015 we were blessed with a fleet of 18, usually there are between nine and a dozen, increasingly sponsored by local businesses.

The 2019 Regatta enjoyed excellent weather. Richard Hews and I had delayed going out in my day boat to watch the racing until 10.45 from an empty harbour. Unfortunately as we were beating out, into a southerly, the Falmouth Working Boats were running in, having had a shortened race, so as to have a break before their 1pm start for the harbour race. We managed to find our way out, tacking without causing any problems, but 10

Red Arrows, Regatta Week

tonnes, travelling at 10 knots, without any brakes and a 20 foot bowspit speaks 'might is right'! 'Victory' sponsored by the RFYC with its striking yellow hull looked magnificent. Our plan was to sail until 12.30 and find a vacant mooring buoy just inside the Castle Point, off Polruan, which is about 50 yards from the southern turning mark. 'Victory' was out early, seeking the most favourable line and tacks through the moorings full of yachts. Equipped with our red wine and sandwiches, this gave us a very good view of the beat from the RFYC start line. With no one over the line, it needed about three tacks up to the castle mark, where the cries of 'starboard' could be heard as they jostled for advantage. At which point, a 40 foot yacht under motor coming from Falmouth, with a view of the race coming towards them for the last five minutes, decided to enter the harbour. She impeded the first four boats on their final tack for the mark and squeezed between Castle Point and our mooring, colliding with moored craft. As she passed our boat we saw the defaced ensign of the Royal Cornwall Yacht Club. As sponsors of the leading impeded boat, I felt obliged to offer advice to the skipper and enquired as to his familiarity with Falmouth Working Boats. Three highly competitive laps were completed several Falmouth Working Boats passing us a few yards west of our stern; 'Victory' was aptly named.

The boats, their crew and singing bring so much to the sailing and atmosphere of the week and it is to be hoped they assemble a large fleet for 2020, their 75th Anniversary. On the Friday a start line was formed 200 yards south of the harbour; a south easterly provided a fair wind back to Falmouth. Farewell to 'main, topsail two foresails and a spinnaker'. For many years we had enjoyed another visiting fleet from Falmouth – Sunbeams, a true and now rare and expensive gentleman's day racer (I sailed in one in the 1980s) – beautiful lines and very low freeboard. The numbers fell away due to a combination of their and their owners age and the difficult passage around the Dodman, where they were vulnerable in the tidal race without an engine.

3. FALSE START

The Day Boat class was based on a few Shrimper 19s, my 17 and my old school friend Bill Wysall's Golant Gaffer (I think only one of two built) plus the odd visiting craft. Handicapping was a much discussed subject, the result was I did reasonably well in light airs but was easily stopped by a bigger swell. From about 2000 we usually had seven entries with five starters each day. Crew came from the office - Jeremy Bailey the most frequent and other friends including a retired Royal Marine.

There was no doubt the Day Boat Class was the 'Ugly Duckling', too slow compared with the Troys and Fowey Rivers and too small for the cruiser classes and the least experienced as regards the racing rules, particularly the starts. In order to ensure we caused the least amount of trouble, we were usually set a single lap course in St Austell Bay with a mark near Par Docks and another off Black Head towards Charlestown, visibility from one to the other being difficult. Whilst this kept our slow progress out of the way, it often resulted in our not completing the course in the prescribed time limit, which was frustrating for skipper and crew.

The Race Officer on the Committee Boat operates on five minute intervals between each stage, during which you need to decipher your class flag, the order of port and starboard race marks, the number of laps and avoid colliding with other boats, looking for the best position on the start line, an imaginary line between the Committee Boat and a buoy about 150 yards away. That year we were starting before the Troys. I had made a bad start but was on good tack so travelled parallel to the start line, as the wind was changing direction. I saw a RIB moving the start buoy away from me so I could not get across. Eventually I tacked but found myself in the middle of twenty or so Troys about to start, some of which offered advice as to where I should go. We managed to complete the inevitable single lap tour of St Austell Bay and in the afternoon took the ferry to the Yacht Club to see the results sheet, where we had been disqualified.

For the afternoon racing the Committee Boat was moored on the Albert Quay Pontoon and I was able to find the Race Officer to enquire as to my misdemeanour. I was told my start was too slow and I had committed the crime of delaying the start of the Troys. I explained I understood his problem and why he needed to adjust the start buoy due to the change in direction of the wind but he had impeded my start and he could not disqualify me before I had started. He took the view that this was such a novel explanation that I was reinstated. Fortunately so few of the Day Boats completed the course I was able to collect some glass ware at prizegiving that evening at the Club.

Unfortunately it gets worse. On what turned out to be the very last year of the Day Boats in 2014 due to lack of numbers, the wind dropped when I was close to the finish line. The time limit for the race had elapsed so I took down the sails and was just starting the engine when the Committee Boat pulled alongside – a bit of a surprise. The Race Officer said as we had been sailing for so long he thought he would bring the finish line to us as we were the only boat left in the class.

So that was a bit of a false finish but luckily more glass wear to collect. Despite efforts, attaching an invitation to join in on suitable craft, we were unable to raise the minimum number of entries the following year. The class was comprised of boats from Polruan and this really tells yet another consequence of 100 letting cottages and fewer families keeping the typical day boat in commission, with the ever widening choice of cheap holidays overseas and the annual cost of mooring, storage, insurance and maintenance of engine and boat.

4. BUTCHER, BAKER, CANDLESTICK MAKER

I have no doubt that 100 years ago there were 40 commercial premises in Polruan. My recollection is 16 and I have indicated their current use, where a change has occurred.

Location	1988	2019
Quay	Shop	No change
West Street	Shop	Cottage
Fore Street (South)	Café	No change
	Shop	Cottage
	Café	Cottage
	Shop	Cottage
	Shop	Cottage
	Restaurant	Cottage
	Post Office	Cottage
Fore Street (North)	Shop	Estate Agents
	Baker	Cottage
	Shop	House
	Butcher	Bakery
	Shop	No change
Top of hill	Co-op	House
	Garage	House

Of course 100 years ago, the emphasis would have been on workshop, rather than shops and it is not difficult to identify properties that were likely to have been used for such purposes. Much has changed in my own recollection since 1960 when the ferry fare was 40p. I think the school had a roll of around 50, now around 30. There were a few privately run letting cottages then, now the largest agent has around 60 and there are probably 100 in total. When I walk down Fore Street on a winter's evening, there are lights on in less than a third of the cottages.

In the 1960s only 5% of school leavers went to University; now it is 50% with degrees of varying quality and relevance to the real world. Those young people then stay in the metropolitan world, changing jobs quite frequently with international experience. All rural and coastal communities are deprived of the more able young and locally owned businesses are few in number. Volunteering falls on the shoulders of ever fewer older people and employment is seasonal in low paid jobs. Nothing is for ever and no one is to blame.

Polruan's strength, its attractiveness is largely due to isolation (much like the Scottish Islands) but that is also its weakness. The white delivery van, with four logos on it has replaced the trading schooner. A photograph of 1901 taken from the Hall Walk shows eight larger trading schooners of 800 tonnes or more, at least 25 large fishing boats, several large yachts and a couple of steam tugs. All creating work in the boatyards and the seaborne trade of all goods filling the shops which in turn serviced the trading schooners. Modern fishing techniques and international markets have replaced the many involved in small boats fishing under sail. What had been a tough but sustainable economy for several hundred years probably failed in the late 1950s.

To illustrate the Butcher in the title, I was giving expert evidence at a Valuation Tribunal in Plymouth and at the end of the first day, Counsel and I adjourned to his hotel for some restorative spirits to review the day and how we would conclude the following day. We finished at about 7pm and as the Tribunal did not start again until 10.30 am and it was a good summers evening, my assistant and I drove down to Polruan for the night. We walked down from the car park and sat in the garden with the last of the sun, then down to the quay and to the Lugger to find a quiet pub and the kitchen having just shut.

Whilst I was relying on the shop to open at 7.30am to provide breakfast, the cupboard was bare at the cottage and morale was low. At which point standing next to me at the bar I was told ' We can't have you with nothing to eat. Come to my butcher's shop and we will find a mixed grill for you'. The shop, now known as Crumpets Two, still has the butchers marble display shop front. We were provided with all the components of a mixed grill at a very reasonable price. My assistant was impressed; I was relieved and his report back in the office improved my standing. Of course this is just one incident but it said a lot about the village.

Polruan still manages to put on a summer and winter play in the Village Hall, holds a church fete and has an

August Bank Holiday Carnival. In the late 1980s our children entered the Fancy Dress competition as residents of Camelford, covered in large green spots based on the pollution of the water supply by two tons of aluminium sulphate, of which we now know the longterm consequences for the population; certainly not politically correct today. There is much more to the Carnival than the Fancy Dress Parade; perhaps the most unusual feature is the Ball Roll – over 1000 numbered tennis balls are 'sold off' and once Fore Street has been cleared, they are released at the top of the hill. Side alleys, drains and steps take their toll as the tidal wave of tennis balls sweeps down the hill, pursued by children and dogs, with prizes for the first arrivals. Its the equivalent to the more familiar duck race and some do end up in the harbour. The all day event starts with the crowning of the Carnival Queen, followed by various competitions and a disco in the Coal Wharf in the evening, now with the benefit of its awning if necessary.

Due to its position and isolation, the National Coast Watch Institution with its many volunteers has taken over the old Coastguard Watch house. There is still a Coastguard Cliff Rescue Unit which depends so critically on local knowledge. Their call outs are usually to livestock and dogs that have gone over the cliff. Also to visitors trapped by the rising tide. Whilst the main beach at Lantic Bay has access to the cliff path, the three coves to the west are all cut off at high tide; locally known as a good place to take ones girlfriend! There is a relatively new Fire and Rescue Station, as Lostwithiel and Looe can easily be half an hours drive away. Thankfully the Post Office function transferred to the

Polruan Carnival, Ball Roll

Polruan Carnival Parade

Winkle Picker shop on the quay providing a much needed cash service, particularly in the summer, as Fowey now has no banks and just one cash machine which can run out in the summer.

As with most villages in Cornwall, Methodism virtually died in a generation by 2000 with so many houses now called The Old Chapel. In the Church of England one priest is responsible for seven churches in the five villages from Polruan to Talland in the Diocese of Cornwall, one of the most financially vulnerable in the country.

St Wyllow, at the head of Pont Pill earns two stars in Simon Jenkins' book 'England's Thousand Best Churches'. His two sentences 'Those who can find this church deserve a medal' and ' there must have been no shortage of parishioners' says it all about rural depopulation from prior to the industrial revolution when around 80% of the population worked on the land as to 3% today. A congregation of around 20, other than on festival days, struggles to sustain a church built for 300.

5. EMERGENCY

I reached Polruan one summer's evening and was soon in the garden with a can of beer, enjoying the sunset over the Gribbin – all was right with the world. I then heard a low call for help which took some time to locate in a nearby garden. There was an elderly lady in a distressed state, badly sunburnt and unable to get out of a folding aluminium chair where the fabric had broken. I called a neighbour but we were unable to get her out of the chair. Other than giving her water, there was nothing else we could do. So we called the local volunteer Fire and Rescue Service, based at the top of the hill. They arrived promptly in their specially designed small engine and quickly cut her free, assessed her condition, gave her oxygen and made her as comfortable as possible on the patio.

They decided she was in urgent need of hospital care and an ambulance was called but we were told none were available as they were all queued up at Derriford in Plymouth and Treliske in Truro. The nearest available ambulance was at the small station in Tavistock which would take one and a half hours to arrive. The decision was taken to call a First Responder from St Austell, an hour by road. Polruan's isolation, its strength and its weakness, was becoming apparent. The car ferry was held in Fowey to overcome that problem. On its arrival Fore Street was now blocked by two vehicles and had been for an hour and a half.

The ambulance arrived two and a half hours after I had discovered our neighbour. It was now dark and like many gardens in Polruan, there was no easy access to the road. We could not use a stretcher as the only route out was down a path, then two flights of steps with tight turns, then through a tunnel under the cottage into Fore Street. It needed all present to manhandle the patient on the folding ambulance chair to the ambulance and transfer her to a stretcher. She spent 10 days in hospital and made a slow recovery. Fore Street had been blocked for three hours from 7pm to 10pm without warning, so the village had been effectively closed.

Those familiar with the normal traffic of cars and light vans at the 'dead end' junction of Fore Street are generally sanguine. This can be daunting for visitors, particularly after six hours driving with 'Are we there yet?' enquiries from children, when confronted by a concrete mixer lorry and not knowing what to do.

6. WHO PAYS THE FERRYMAN

We were booked in at the RFYC for dinner with Lynn and Tony Bartlett (I had a half share in an Enterprise dinghy with Tony in the 1960s) so we took the 7pm ferry over to Fowey, aware that it ran until 11pm which 'gave us plenty of time'.

Royal Fowey Yacht Club

It was a long and slow dinner and due to human failings we got to Town Quay to see the last ferry gone. We returned to the Club to consider our position. Prior to mobile phones there was a coin operated phone booth then, so taxi via Lostwithiel was an option but it was a nice calm evening and the club tender was on the frape. This could take two of us but as evening became morning we discovered this required five trips. Tony and I rowed to Polruan, went to our cellar, got my tender and two horse power outboard and set off from the beach towing the club tender.

We could then use my tender to tow the club tender, which could take three if no one was rowing, and it stayed calm and I went slowly. Our wives' morale was falling, it is cold and damp at midnight on the river and pitch black on the club slipway and 'slip' was a distinct possibility in their evening footwear. The harbour was full of boats and mooring lines and we had no torch.

This was my third crossing of the river and I was very relieved to get to the ferry steps in Polruan. We were all cold and went up to the cottage to warm up. All that was left to do was for me to tow the club tender back to its mooring and then bring my tender back and push my way towards a ladder on the quay and climb up with my painter and add it to the many on the eye ring. A pontoon would have made life a lot easier. We were pleased with our initiative on the night but recognised we had taken too many risks.

This reminds me of the 'right of passage' for children leaving the Primary School and going on to the Secondary School in Fowey. With the benefit of the proper support and right conditions, they celebrate this by swimming from Polruan to Town Quay – until you get in the water you don't appreciate how far this is.

Many years ago before swimming pools, the two coves outside of the Castle were designated as the boys and girls coves.

Similarly for the Triathlon athletes who in early September, start with a swim from Fowey, run dripping up to the Coal Wharf in Polruan to retrieve their bikes. They then face over 300 feet up Fore Street, then down to Pont, back up to Highway down again to Pen Poll, up and down again to Lerryn and along the east bank to Lostwithiel and beyond with a run back via Par.

7. UP RIVER

The most important practical element of 'Sailing from Polruan' is the pontoon, installed in the 1990s. Prior to this there were a few frapes to the south of the quay but most tenders were moored with a long painter north of the quay. You forced your way through other tenders, then climbed the ladder holding the line to find an eye ring full of other lines, all of which looked the same.

We used to stay at Pont Farmhouse in the early 1980s and the National Trust supplied a boat with an outboard. For the shopping trip to Polruan, it was easier to land on the beach and keep an eye on the tide. Indeed the tide has a very different meaning when going down river than up river.

The river offers much and many families hire a boat with a five or six horse power outboard for the week. All you need to do is find the way upriver and understand the tides. So perhaps this chapter should be called 'Boating from Polruan'.

With springs 5.7m high and 0.3m low, there can be tides of three knots at the harbour entrance and from the vehicle ferry to Golant, as the great basin north of Golant fills and drains. The significance of that is that with a typical five knot engine, the results over the ground with the tide, eight knots; against the tide two knots, planning your trip is everything. Also high water can vary from 4m to 5.7m or five and a half feet.

To get the most from 'up river' with say two hours ashore, start for Golant two hours before high water; Lerryn just under two and half hours before and Lostwithiel only on springs, say two and three quarter hours before. The reason is you have a strong tide, no need to rush and should you go aground, there is still plenty of 'lift'. Coming back, leave no later than half an hour after high water. This means there is not much tidal 'drop' so its easy to sort yourself out if you go aground. Lastly if you are in a sailing boat with a lifting centre plate, don't lift it up to start with as it's the best guide to shallow water and as you lift it up, so you keep going.

All Aboard for 'Up River'

Our Drascombe Lugger was made for the job, drawing only one foot with the plate up but you did need to remove the rudder which could jam. The Crabber 17 drew two feet with the plate and rudder up and was not capable of carrying oars which are particularly useful. Sailing beyond the car ferry can best be described as 'flukey' and difficult in the swinging moorings beyond the docks. However using just the roller jib, it was easy to adjust and permitted motor sailing. More often than not the wind was blowing up river and dropped around 7pm

Lerryn Quay ' Up River'

There are six very differing choices, some totally dependant on tide. Pont, the easiest, can be a problem as a strong easterly or westerly accelerates in the steep valley to the east. The last third of the creek is shallow but well worth the effort to land on the quay at Pont Farmhouse, once a pub. Beyond the car ferry, the small creek of Mixstow, little changed for 45 years after the war where it had been the base for a flotilla of six motor gunboats, capable of 40knots, one of the skippers being Sir Peter Scott.

FHC purchased some land from what was known as Yeate Farm in about 2000. Over the years they have provided extensive pontoons and later a large workshop and sales to create a boatyard with the storage area. In recent years Mixstow has been renamed Penmarlem. Best of all, the day time café at the top of the pontoon bridge becomes a delightful bistro in the evenings.

Golant, a mile up river on the west bank, is easy, until you get to the steps on the short quay. You need to squeeze in by the boathouse and get someone ashore with long lines, as there are limited eye rings, then move the boat along the quay so others can land and as usual, plenty of fenders are needed. The Fishermans Arms is three hundred yards up the road. We once went up too early in the Crabber and went aground; after a quick brew up we were able to reach the quay.

The last three require a bit more thought. Penpoll, to the east, is a mile long and shallow, so little visited – a haven for waders including curlew, little egret and on the northern bank there are two decoy nests on poles to attract ospreys on migration. I have been up the creek half a dozen times and reached the conclusion that slowly up the middle on a good tide is the best way. On my last trip with Richard Hews in his Pioneer 14, with lifting engine, we decided that being able to read the finger board on the signpost by the bridge was the proper test of success.

The last two benefit from taking the walk through the woods from Lerryn to St Winnow. Not only is there St Winnow Church to enjoy which featured in the original TV series of Poldark, the farmer's wife Angie runs an excellent burger bar there in the summer. The 1:25,000 Ordnance Survey Sheet SX05/15 is very useful as charting what you see on your walk.

As you enter the Lerryn River, hug the east bank and then slowly work your way across to the west bank where a creek appears in front of you. Then straight down the middle, going close to the quay and converted building on the south bank, then swing across tight to the converted building on the north bank, avoiding the large mud bank to starboard. There is a useful quay on the south bank; at high water springs you get your feet wet. The pub The Ship and an excellent shop which also serves coffee as well as being the Post Office, is two hundred yards away.

Now you have completed your apprenticeship, time for the six miles up to Lostwithiel on a spring tide. From the entrance to the Lerryn river, take the east bank for about one third of a mile then to the middle of the river where the railway crosses over a creek, then closer to the railway, then hug the slipway just beyond the church. The rest of the way, up the middle of the river. Keep right as a finger of Shirehall Moor narrows the river which then meanders for three quarters of a mile through Madderly Moor marsh with plenty of wildlife to be seen. If you have a mast, either lower it or moor at the newish quay on the west bank. This has good ladders and plenty of eye rings. You will see this is where the Fowey China Clay line branches off the main line. After a quarter of a mile through the park, where you are very much in a river, under the low railway bridge past the railway workshops converted to residential and you are at the medieval quay. Lostwithiel was a port until the China Clay industry silted up the whole river. Its probably worth turning round now, as if other boats come up, it gets tight.

You are now in the centre of the town where tea shops, fish and chips, restaurants and four pubs, two south of the main road and two to the north, including The Globe, the nearest, are all available for two hours only. If you are moored at the southern end of the park, you have less than two hours! Going back is much easier as you are at the top of the tide and know the way. An alternative approach is to loiter at the entrance of the Lerryn river when tripper boats have been advertised and follow them up river but you will have to queue at the fish and chip shop!

The only mishap we have had over 30 years and perhaps 50 trips up river was at Lerryn, which for several reasons is the most popular. We had gone up with the children and dog in our Drascombe Lugger. As my wife got out of the boat on the quay, her keys slipped out of her pocket and fell into the one inch gap between the boat and the quay. We came back the following day at low water and found them in the mud. The trip was fated; as we were ready to go back to Polruan at dusk the dog got disorientated swimming and could not be retrieved. Fortunately Bertie Ellis was also up river in his more manoeuvrable Dory and caught up with him.

When you get to Lostwithiel for the first time and leave within the prescribed time, there is time to stop at Golant for up to an hour, to celebrate your achievement. With any luck at the weekend there will be a band playing on the covered stage overlooking the inner harbour at the Fishermans Arms – an hour can pass very quickly.

In conclusion, with good weather and a spring tide, the trip to Lostwithiel with a short stop at Golant and the café/bistro at Penmarlam on the way back makes a wonderful six hours. This gives a new perspective of the river as you pass from coast through estuary and marsh to inland river. The remarkable seclusion, eco-system and if you look carefully, its previous role since medieval times as a highway with several small quays underpinning the social life and the economy.

8. LANTIC BAY

Over the last ten years the Sunday paper supplements have been full of best walks, best pubs etc and worst of all, best secret beaches. Lantic Bay was soon much reported but recently Lansallos Church Cove has also been 'discovered' a mile to the east round Pencarrow Head.

Shortly after university, our elder daughter Laura invited five friends to stay in our tiny cottage which has an average width of ten feet and few beds, I said I would pop down, on a good day and be their boatman and sleep on the boat.

The three boys decided to go to Carlyon Bay to play golf and the three girls would have a beach day. The only decent beach on the Polruan side being Lantic Bay. I took them round towing my eight foot tender to anchor off and row them ashore. My mistake was to anchor off Lantic, rather than Little Lantic to the east with its protection from the swell.

It was perfect – sunny and no wind and I anchored 100 yards off and rowed Laura ashore, save for the last five yards where we waded ashore from the upturned tender, soaked! Despite best efforts I could not row back through the short breaking waves. All Laura could do was climb the 300ft cliff and walk back to Polruan. The two girls in the boat, enjoying the sun were unaware of our problem and no other boats had yet arrived in the bay. In these circumstances, you feel there is something you should do. I could swim back and explain what had happened; but I could not row back because as soon as you put a foot in the tender, with a wave it capsized. I decided to tie the painter to my ankle and tow the empty and light tender through the waves.

They were somewhat surprised to see me and I explained that Laura was fine but that we ought to go back. Luckily I kept a small rope ladder in the cockpit to get back on board and we sailed back. As the day went on, boats did arrive, some with inflatable tenders, which would have solved the problem rather more easily. After their holiday one of the girls sent me a postcard of thanks for the use of the cottage and how much she had enjoyed the trip to Lantic Bay – little did she know!

The plan for the evening was to go up to Lerryn but with seven of us in the boat, water started coming up the drain in the self- draining cockpit. Not wishing to leave anyone behind, I advanced the theory that with the engine at full speed it would give the hull 'lift' and we would be all right – luckily this worked and we had a wonderful evening.

For those who have read 'The Salt Path', in the top ten for non- fiction for much of 2018 and 2019, there is a page towards the end when the author has completed the south west coast path meets 'Robert' on the path above Lantic Bay. Their conversation is based on a

Seven 'Up River' after Lantic Bay

sparrow hawk, which can often be seen performing its aerobatics and for those who know 'Robert' you can hear his voice in those words. For as long as I know 'Robert' has lived in his timber shack with a few chickens, completely off grid below the path to Carne Beach just above the entrance to Pont Pill.

9. POLPERRO

Coming out of Pont Pill through the visitors moorings, I saw the new Moody that my partner Roger and his wife Janet had bought after selling me his Drascombe. Over a cup of tea on board I agreed to take them up river to Lerryn and call at Golant on the way back. They offered me a sail the following day back to Plymouth and I suggested they drop me off at Polperro and I would find my own way back. They picked me up from the pontoon – I was travelling light – towel, swimming trunks and bottle of water.

With relatively light winds force 2/3 and some motoring we cruised close to the coast, Lantic Bay, Pencarrow Head with the old coastguards lookout over Lantivit Bay, a stunning Lansallos Church Cove, a favourite of the smugglers using a cart track cut through the cliff. Then several miles of deeply incised cliff and the disused sheltered south facing cliff gardens of Polperro came into view. In the early 1960s I remember donkeys with panniers still being used to carry flowers and vegetables along the cliff path down to the village.

By the mid 1960s my parents were living permanently at Polperro in the 'Watchers' on the cliff (a name given to Customs and Excise in the nineteenth century). When I sat in bed I could watch the Eddystone Lighthouse. The house shared a path with a large 1920s house called 'Seaways'; the principal reception room of which was double height with a first floor gallery and bedrooms off. Rita Tushingham had just bought it with the proceeds of Dr Zhivago and The Knack, both released in 1965.

I was a student in London and at the end of term, waiting at Paddington Station, the holidays had begun once the tannoy announced all the stations after Plymouth, when the fast train became a slow train. I wish I had been able to attend the parties at Seaways, the 1960s was quite a time. During the summer vacations I worked nights on the fishing boats which landed their catch at Polperro about 6am and was then loaded into a van for the fish market in Looe.

We rounded Peak Rock with one of the tightest deep harbour entrances on the south coast facing south east and so sheltered from the prevailing westerlies. There are several large mooring buoys, 100 yards south of the inner harbour; its narrow entrance is protected by timber baulks with a crane. The harbour dries and is fairly full of boats. It is probably best to moor on the buoys and hail a passing tripper boat to put you ashore. Polperro remains one of the most attractive small harbours, with narrow streets, minimal vehicular access and two good pubs -The Blue Peter and The Three Pilchards. This was a centre for smuggling with narrow alleys, interconnected cottages and access to the small river at high tide. The village flooded very badly, similar to Boscastle, in 1976 and again in 1993. The only solution was a tunnel, dug from a mile upstream to create an overflow which runs out through the cliff to the west of the village.

It is a tough 6 miles, three hours plus coast path walk to Polruan with at one point in Lantivet Bay 157 steps. I retraced my youthful route by road to Lansallos and walked down the track to the beach to swim and some sun. By mid afternoon, time to return, to avoid the cliff path I went back up the track to the Church. A couple in a fairly old car pulled alongside. They were lost and were looking for Polruan. I explained it was complicated but would be pleased to guide them in their car. Ten minutes later they were parked in the main car park and we walked down the hill to the cottage for tea in the garden.

10. ST AUSTELL BAY

The Bay is perhaps seen as the 'Ugly Sister' as far as cruisers are concerned; they are either on passage or racing to finish and get back to the bar and generally disfigured by the China Clay works at Par. For the small boat there are five harbours; three require you to round the Gribbin whereas the other two are farther west.

Polridmouth, before the Gribbin, is the same distance as Lantic Bay but is much less busy and less subject to the noise and danger of jet skis and water skiers. Nice anchorage and swimming but worth having a look at low water to see there are two beaches. My first landing was in the early 90s. I had invited a couple of the graduates in the office for a weekend sailing. Yes, said four; I explained there were not enough beds. They reassured me, not to worry.

We arrived on Friday evening. The two girls took over the attic and the boys agreed with me that there were not enough beds. However, they converted the summer house with cushions. On Saturday morning we went to Yeate Farm (Penmarlem) to launch the Drascombe, only to find the rudder was missing. This is a very distinctive item – rudder, vertical shaft and tiller 'all in one'. It slots into a housing like a centre plate in the small aft deck, forward of the outboard well.

Though we could motor, we could not sail but as we chatted, a possible ancient solution emerged. By lashing an oar to the slot for the bumpkin a stearboard (or starboard) was created in the style of the Viking longboats. In light airs this worked and we beached a couple of hours before low water. Once they were ashore with dry feet, I threw the anchor as far out as possible and with the bow on a frape gently tugged the boat out and secured that by a long line. They had noticed the Day Mark and we climbed the 300 feet and celebrated with the cans they were pleased were in my bag. With low tide at midday, we were able to go up river to Golant for the evening. They were fortunate with the tide and weather. I was less fortunate as a few weeks later I had to go to South Devon for a replacement 'all in one', where I heard the dreaded words 'it will have to be specially made'.

'All in One' rudder, St Austell Bay

Behind the trees at the top of the valley is Menabilly, Daphne du Maurier's old house and the model for Manderley. It is impossible not to sail past and think of Rebecca and the boat house. Less known is that during the war there were large metal trays beyond the beach that could be filled with petrol and set on fire as a decoy to attract German bombers away from the docks. Fowey played an important role preparing American landing craft crews for D Day and subsequently, as a major port for shipping munitions, stored in depots around Bodmin.

The moment you round Gribbin and Cannis, where you can really see the tide, any northerly wind has had two miles in which to change sea conditions. Polkerris, two miles to the north, with its old pilchard cellars, the Rashleigh Arms and Sams on the Beach has a short quay and at low water it is difficult to moor alongside. My last visit was when the wind dropped at the racing mark near Par Docks and we adjourned for swimming.

Par is now a closed commercial port and charmless in all respects. I was once asked to advise a consortium on the feasibility of a marina in the docks. I was shown a layout with boats moored stern on. I explained we enjoyed an 18 foot rise and fall. It was explained that their client liked it how it was in the Mediterranean, where there was a couple of feet rise and fall. The consequential contaminated land clean up costs exceeded the value of the marina many times over.

Charlestown is really worth a visit for many reasons. It was the original china clay port, a lovely late Georgian model village which accounts for its starring role in films and its stock of square rigged sailing ships. The only problem I have had is high quay walls and distant securing points – two on board helps.

In theory Mevagissey is attractive with a large accessible harbour. It is full of fishing boats and difficult to moor alongside. Also it is the south of Cornwall capital of fish and chips. I can well see why tourists catch the ferry from Mevagissey.

Gorran Haven is an attractive village with a drying harbour. Here I have had my first and hopefully my last, mishap with an anchor which I had dropped at half tide, only to watch the end of the chain disappear over the bow. I beached the boat, waited for low tide and walked out across the harbour dragging my feet to retrieve the chain. I suppose most of us do this once but the visit turned into a seven hour stay. You are now only a mile from the Dodman where 23 adults and 8 children on board a pleasure boat from Falmouth, The Darlwyne, perished in heavy seas the same weekend that England won the football World Cup in 1966. The tidal race can stretch several miles out to sea and requires a great deal of respect.

Once in St Austell Bay, with some mist, rain or poor light, the significance of the Day Mark is very apparent. I have been caught in a sudden fog once – it is totally disorientating. Usually there is little wind so on with the engine, having taken a bearing on Fowey harbour entrance beforehand, estimate how far away it is and which way you will turn if you can't find it.

11. HELFORD

Although I have sailed round the Iberian Peninsula, from Cornwall to the Western Isles, in New Zealand, to the Solent for 'Round the Island Race', my favourite remains Polruan to Falmouth, particularly beyond to the Helford. Those familiar with David Weston's wonderful 'Epic Onwards', 1995 Circumnavigation of Cornwall in a Mirror Dinghy will already have got the message! I have been there several times with Tony Edwards in his Swan 37 'Ondina of Polruan', a wonderful sea boat. Due to fog we failed to get round the Lizard but walked the north and south sides of the Helford River.

The river is unique for many reasons. Though short, it cuts three quarters of the way across the Lizard, making the south bank beyond Gweek, isolated with wonderful walking to the point and back via Gillan Creek to Helford Village. The north bank enjoys a microclimate with magnificent classic Cornwall Spring gardens at Trebah, still with its wartime slips for D day landing ships and Glendurgan, both with lovely beaches. Helford Passage on the north bank is a small and very attractive village with the Ferryboat Inn, good beach facilities and has the seasonal ferry service. This can be delayed at low water due to limited access at Helford

Village. During the War the river was a base for the Secret Service. landing agents in France, using French fishing boats with powerful engines, enabling them to be far from the French coast in day light hours.

At the head there is the small village of Gweek, with its boatyard, accessible only at high water. This was one of the more unusual boatyards/marinas I valued over a period of 30 years.

In 1988 I bought the classic Drascombe Lugger from a partner in our firm and secured an annual mooring on the outer trot at the RFYC, one of forty the Club leased from FHC. After a year or two I decided I could sail there on my own, the principle being you wait for a northerly or an easterly on the basis there will always be a westerly along fairly soon to get you home. Drascombes are really at their best in an estuary due to a shallow draft of one foot with the plate up. With a loose footed main they run well but this limits their ability to beat into the wind.

As a totally open boat they can take in water when beating but this lies in the side deck seats and runs out again as you change tack. A pair of oars is very cleverly stowed in the sides, the small demountable mizzen mast is very handy and some people have sailed them thousands of miles.

The most extraordinary being Ken Duxbury in the 1970s in the Scilly Isles and Western Isles and as recorded in his book 'Lugworm Homeward Bound' from Greece to England in an Open Boat. The voyage took from April to October in 1972. Not only was he a brilliant sailor but also a great observer and reporter of the engagement of people with nature, way ahead of the nature travel writers of the last fifteen years.

The trip hinges on having slack water at the Dodman, nine miles from Polruan so as to be able to creep round the headland and avoid the tidal race which can extend several miles to the south. Helford is a good twenty miles away, whilst a cruiser in favourable conditions might be thinking about four hours, a Drascombe should plan for six hours and should not sail in wind strength above force four. Whilst working full time in Bristol, such a trip was inevitably opportunistic rather than planned, as ideally you want several days to play with. After Mevagissey there is no harbour beyond the Dodman until Falmouth.

I think it was in 1991 that I started in light airs with the five horse power outboard providing a steady four knots, three hours before high water which gave ideal conditions for rounding the Dodman. The wind picked up, past Caerhays Castle, Gull Rock and Nare Head and Zone Point comes into view with its lighthouse and the wonderful and welcome Carrick Roads.

I had a bed booked in St Mawes, found a buoy and used the usual technique of asking a passing tender to put me ashore. The following day I sailed the four miles across Falmouth Bay, avoiding August Rock to the north east of the entrance to the river and had dinner at the thatched Shipwrights Arms in Helford Village. For the first and last time I slept in the bottom of the boat with the sail on top but there is no beating the damp cold at 2am in the morning. True to form you never need to wait long for a westerly. I allowed four hours for slack water at the Dodman as it is easier to slow down than speed up.

As is often the case when you approach a major headland, the wind strengthens and changes direction. What had been a comfortable run became, single handed, an unmanageable beat. So down came the main and up with the mizzen mast. I set up the bumpkin (the opposite of a bowsprit) and with the jib and mizzen alone, orderly Drascombe sailing was restored. The Daymark was a very welcome sight as it is impossible to identify Fowey Harbour from nine miles away; compass bearings are not much use when you are beating.

Ten years later I bought a new Crabber 17 (now known as Shrimper 17), the same length as the Lugger but a much heavier and powerful boat with a large boomed main and most important of all, a covered foredeck, into which two full length berths are squeezed and a self-draining cockpit. This coincided with a fore and aft FHC mooring becoming available in Pont Pill, both sheltered and beautiful.

This was the year of the total eclipse and I recall sailing a few miles south of the harbour, darkness, all the seagulls landing in the sea, a stillness at about 11am and then the light from the west. After a couple of years getting to know the boat, it was time for Helford. This time a bunk, with plenty of water, some cans, fruit, handy eating and tea and milk for the single burner gas stove in the cockpit.

Solar Eclipse, St Austell Bay 11am on 11/08/1999

Following my earlier trip in the Drascombe, the drill of wait for a northerly, with the wind off the land (more comfortable than an easterly) worked well to the Dodman but the wind dropped later in the day and as I wanted to get up the River Fal, a couple of hours with the five horse power engine got me from Nare Head to Zone Point, the entrance to Carrick Roads. My plan was to get half way to Truro, past St Mawes and its Castle, Falmouth and the National Trust Trelissick House, where the river narrows. On with the engine to get past the King Harry Car Ferry and its chains and the large cargo vessels in storage and fish farms.

Smugglers Cottage is a mile up river on the eastern bank with an excellent pontoon; the pub could also be accessed down a concrete road built for D Day boarding. (On more recent visits sadly the pub is now a private house). This provided my evening meal and a mooring for the night. On the western bank the large National Trust estate of Trelissick includes Round Wood Quay, used in the nineteenth century for the export of minerals and now totally vacant. It is easy to moor up and walk up to the prehistoric fort, one of the very few esturine forts in the South West. I spent a leisurely morning sailing across to the Pandora Inn at Mylor which has a pontoon of 100 yards or so equipped with tables and chairs for lunch. (This building was subsequently burnt down but has been well restored).

In the afternoon I sailed the six miles across Falmouth Bay to Port Navas about half way along the north bank of the Helford River. I found a buoy, had a cup of tea and reflected on my cold night at Smugglers Cottage. I had failed to put up the canopy on an aluminium frame which forms a small tent over the forward cockpit. This keeps the warmth in and the summer dew out. Dinner was an inevitable 'boil in the bag'; apple; cheese and red wine followed by coffee and Radio 4. At two o'clock in the morning the boat lurched 20 degrees to starboard and tipped me out of the bunk. I had failed to wind the steel centre plate up. If I had, the boat would have gently grounded on the falling tide but the plate had held it up until gravity took control.

Breakfast – cereal, a roll and coffee - and I took advantage of the rising tide to motor up to Gweek Boatyard which had once been the port for Helston. It houses a remarkable collection of 'sole trader' craftsmen who can make and repair almost any craft up to about 60 ft in length. The falling tide took me down to Frenchmen's Creek on the south bank about half a mile up river from Helford Village. It speaks Daphne du Maurier and reminded me of her book which we had seen re-enacted on a ship moored at the head of Pont Pill, with cannons on the lime kilns during the May Fowey Festival.

I finished the day on Helford Sailing Club's long pontoon with the plate up drawing just under two feet, with good food and company and the benefit of the canopy for my third night. I had avoided any mooring fees with good weather but cold nights and left early in the morning, with little wind so motored east at four knots for the Dodman. As usual by 10am there was some wind – westerly – and I reached the Dodman after four or so hours at slack water. The wind increased and I knew I had to get both reefs in the main secured quickly – with one pair of hands this is not easy. A passing yacht saw I was struggling and stood by as I tried to keep the boat head to the wind, get the reefs in and reset the main, having previously roller reefed the jib. It was a difficult ten minutes.

There were plenty of white horses and wind strength of a good force five. The boat ran at its fastest ever and Dodman to Fowey was a quick hour and a half. I was very relieved to come head into wind, get the sails down and just drift for a few minutes up to Pont. With a couple of minutes of engine I was on the fore and aft mooring, a cup of tea and sleep.

12. SCILLY

We first went to the Isles of Scilly in about 1985 on a day trip on the Scillonian and since then have gone most years, in Spring or Autumn, taking the dogs with us. If the Scillies were in the Western Isles there would be two Caledonian McBrae, roll on roll off ferries 365 days of the year rather than a 40 year old seasonal pedestrian ferry and flights very vulnerable to storms and fog. However, inaccessibility has enabled the Islands to retain their beauty, simplicity and character.

Sunset, Western Isles from Star Castle, Scilly

Despite several attempts to get there with Tony Edwards in Ondina of Polruan, we never got round the Lizard due to fog. An opportunity arose in 1991 to sail a Moody 36, centre cockpit, when the owner was at his son's wedding, with Tony Bartlett as Skipper and Chris Jones and I as crew. Moodys are best known for comfort rather than performance with a big saloon and large fore and aft cabins.

We left Fowey late on a Thursday evening at the start of September, the course to the Scillies is broadly southwest and the lighthouses handed us on, as if we were a baton in a relay race:

Eddystone, capable of being seen for 40 miles, to our east, 20 miles away;

St Anthonys, Falmouth;

Lizard, passed at 05.30 hours in a good force 3. Tony and I had last struggled round here in 1973 in his small cruiser.

Tater Du, south of Penzance;

Longships, one mile west of Lands End;

Wolf Rock, eight miles south west of Lands End;

Seven Stones Lightship, eight miles north west of Lands End

Bishop Rock, west of the Scillies.

Round Island, north of the Scillies

There were always lighthouses in view whose changing bearing gave a sense of progress – night sailing at its best. It was a relatively easy night sail with two of us in the cockpit trying to work out the position and direction of fishing boats from their navigation lights.

This was my most memorable night sail since the age of 16 when I sailed from Sussex to the Channel Islands in a Hillyard, a nine tonne double ended centre cockpit motor-sailer with a school friend and his father. We got to Alderney, behind the old Victorian Admiralty breakwater but due to the swell could not get off the boat for 3 days!

In daylight the course to the Scillies is marked by the steady flow of helicopters and fixed wing aircraft, not to mention the Scillonian on her morning passage to St Marys.

The Author and Tony Bartlett, Scilly

We took the northern route past Round Island and anchored between Tresco and Bryher with Hangman's Hill to the west and Cromwell Castle to the east the two main features. This must be one of the most beautiful anchorages in Southern England. Lunch, red wine, sleep.

Moody 36 between Bryher and Tresco

In the afternoon we went to Tresco for the Garden, still perhaps the most impressive in the UK with plants from all over the world, to be followed by dinner at the New Inn. This meant inflating the tender, tidying up the boat (forgetting to leave a light for the return trip, more on the problem later).

Our evening at the New Inn was a celebration of our passage, aware of the very favourable conditions we had enjoyed. Returning from the New Inn at 11pm the inflatable was located and as the tide had fallen, carried across the beach, outboard started and away.

Unfortunately the foreshore now comprised a series of shallow lagoons with sand bars and in the dark this became a formidable and wet obstacle as the tender was carried and relaunched on several occasions.

Finally free, we set off, sitting on the wet sides of the inflatable, for where we thought the boat was moored in a line of half a dozen yachts in the narrow channel. The outboard engine spluttered to a halt and the tender struck an unusual angle with bow and stern low in the water. Tony concluded that the crew in the 'portering' had let the painter trail in the water which as we increased speed had come under the hull and tangled with the propeller of the two horse outboard.

Tenders are at the best of times difficult to row but with the bow low in the water forward movement shipped water and we did not know which way to row. Gentle rowing brought us alongside a yacht. We explained our predicament and with only one in the tender Tony was able to get his hand on the prop and untangle the painter. Suitably chastened we worked up the line of boats, many lessons learnt; restored by whisky.

In the morning we went to Bryher landing on Anneka's quay, built as a challenge in an old TV programme and had a pizza at the Fraggle Rock Café, a unique institution. (Bryher is now more sophisticated with the refurbishment of Hell Bay Hotel, graced with the title of one of the best 100 hotels in the world).

We did not visit the other inhabited 'off island' St Martins, a couple of miles north of Tresco, which over the years has become a favourite as it is perhaps the least visited and has a thriving community, a good pub, The Seven Stones, and the most westerly vineyard in the UK.

In the afternoon we motored five miles south to St Agnes. A sand bar runs east west to the small island of Gugh. We anchored on the northern side avoiding the Cow and Calf rock in the middle of Porth Conger, with the potential to sail round Gugh to The Cove as an alternative anchorage if the wind changed.

St Agnes with a permanent population of only 80 would not normally justify a pub. However the campsite and summer visitors keep the Turks Head busy. The pub was run by John and Pauline Dart, Scillonians, who had previously run the Lugger Inn at Polruan. After a walk of about an hour around the island with its many prehistoric features we were warmly received by our old friends. We had perhaps spent too long in the pub since on returning to the quay, the painter to the tender was two feet under the water. We recall seeing a naked blond walking along the sand bar but were not sure if this was before or after we went to the pub.

On the Sunday morning the wind had freshened and was again easterly 4/5 and likely to strengthen. We motored over to St Marys and used the visitor mooring adjacent to the lifeboat. With a population of 2000, St

Marys has all the facilities visiting yachts require. Our previously welcome easterly now meant a long hard beat back to Fowey, setting off to sail through the night using our chain of lights. Our passage was assisted by motor sailing in order to manage tides and achieve courses so as to minimize the effects of the main head-lands. After 20 hours we were back in Fowey, a truly memorable long weekend, indeed the best I can recall.

Some years later, on one of our annual trips across on the Scillonian, Mike Mitchell, the Polruan pilot and previous owner of Troy 11, was also working at his much loved job as Reserve Master. Liz and I were sur-prised to hear over the tannoy 'would Mr and Mrs Stapleton please report to the bridge'. We could not think why and feared the worst but Mike was very keen to show us his 'office' with the best views in the house. He was a great supporter of Gig Racing and explained the challenge of shipping 130 gigs on and off the Scillies each Spring for the World Championships which doub-led the islands' population for a few days. He also told us of his time on the Scillies where his father had been the lighthouse keeper.

On a cold and bright day in December 2019, together with over 200 others, I attended his Memorial Service in Polruan. Mike as a cadet in the Merchant Navy served on the convoys to the Mediterranean and throughout his life had been most friendly and helpful to everyone, including us in 1988 with some storage and a temporary mooring. He was from a generation the like of which we are unlikely to see again.

13. ONDINA OF POLRUAN

A friend of mine, Tony Edwards who had bought a house in Walk Terrace in the 1960s, had a yawl, called Ondina of which I had only seen a photograph. She was probably built in the 1920s and went to her grave in the 1960s. However I still have her heavy canvas mizzen sail which we have been using as an awning in the garden. As we live on the western slopes of Dartmoor, it is more used for protection from the rain rather than the sun. I got to know Tony in the late 1970s and crewed for him for ten years on her replacement Ondina of Polruan, a Swan 37. When I started there were four foresails to be hanked on and no roller reefing which was hard work. Thankfully Tony relented and we went up to Plymouth to have what was quite an expensive piece of kit fitted. On our next trip westwards, we were sailing across Falmouth Bay when the wind gusted from 10 knots to 30 knots in a minute; within another minute we were head to wind, jib reduced in size by half and money very well spent.

The yacht was a classic cruiser/racer known internationally and the complete opposite of the Moody 36 referred to in 'Scilly'. There was no large aft cabin, just the cockpit with deep side lockers under the seats, full of boating gear, a saloon with two settee and a pilot

Tony Edwards, Ondina – note sail bags

berth, a small fore cabin with two tight bunks and limited headroom, all within a slim hull and much lower than the centre cockpit Moody. With a long keel, responsive and in the most favourable conditions, running with a force 5, she was capable of 10 knots (against the Moody, just over 6 knots) and one of the fastest boats I have sailed. Not surprising, since the fastest were a pair of detuned Americas Cup boats left in Auckland after the America's Cup which required 16 crew to operate the winch grinders. Having convinced the skipper you could have ten minutes on the helm. ......speed 20 knots. We occasionally raced in the Cruiser fleet at the start of Regatta Week to Falmouth on Sunday afternoon, moored by Flushing Quay, where the café provided breakfast on Monday morning, racing back to arrive in the afternoon, together with the Falmouth flotilla joining us for the Regatta including the Falmouth Working Boats.

Tony Edwards and family + Author, Ondina.

We also sailed east, Newton Ferrers being a favourite, lining up the marks for what was a difficult entrance into the River Yealm. Once moored on a buoy, there was a small landing point just below the old hotel which had a noisy African Grey parrot in the bar. (Long since closed and converted into flats). Then a footpath to the Dolphin with lovely views from its terrace across to Noss Mayo.

The best weekend was joining the Royal Thames on their summer cruise at Dartmouth, a very social crowd on a Saturday. We met for drinks at the Royal Dart Terrace at Kingswear, then in the afternoon, with the rising tide a boat trip up to Totnes, past Greeenway and Dittisham with a commentary on the estuary. On the way back the commentary was replaced by endless Pimms. There was an hour to smarten ourselves up, blazers and white trousers for dinner up the hill at the Royal Naval College. We had the slowest start to Sunday I can ever remember.

Dartmouth Royal Naval College – off to dinner, Ondina

Tony had set his heart on sailing in 'Round the Island Race' – at its time the largest sailing race in the world with 1200 boats in many different classes from 90 foot round the world racers to 24 foot cruisers. Starting from Cowes, going anti-clockwise round the Isle of Wight which due to its unique location and shape had not two but four tides a day and really required local knowledge. The crew were his son Wayne, Mike Bradshaw, Bob Durie and myself. The delivery plan was to leave Polruan in the evening, guided by the Eddystone lighthouse, making for Weymouth just over 100 miles away. One of my great memories was on the helm at midnight, a few miles off the Eddystone with its beam lighting my course. Once round Portland Bill which was all right, we had a tough couple of hours beating into a northerly, against the tide. With hindsight we should have gone into Portland Harbour with its massive breakwaters.

The following morning, we had an early start for the 80 miles to Cowes. St Albans Head was nearly halfway there, then the Needles and Hurst Castle Spit. Here the Solent is little more than a mile wide with the strongest of tides, which we would be dealing with in the morning. Considerable skill is needed as you enter the harbour quite apart from all the yachts, avoiding the constant ferries, both ships and hydrofoils, I can't remember whether there were hovercraft as well. Here we moored up fore and aft on piles, with ingenious slides for the tides, six or seven boats deep, with a mass of lines to be unravelled in the morning.

On the way to the start we saw Velsheda, a massive J class which had raced in Fowey in the 1930s. Starting without a collision was frenetic and terrifying. As novices our sole aim was to safely complete the course in what I recall was force 4 to 5, ideal conditions. Its about 60 miles around the island. We set off west down the Solent; though we lacked local knowledge of the tides, with 1200 boats and the larger racing yachts ahead of us, it was not difficult to work out where we should be sailing. We put someone in the bow to avoid collisions in the narrows off Hurst Castle. The wind was lighter on the southern side of the island and the style for us was more like cruising, followed by a beat up Spithead, past the old defensive forts to the finish. We had quite a sense of achievement; Tony produced champagne and caviar, reminding us that 'any bloody fool can be uncomfortable'.

Last time I looked, Mike Slade (I was with him at The College of Estate Management in the 1960s) held the

Velsheda, Round the Island Race

record for the fastest circumnavigation in a mono hull Leopard, in near perfect conditions of under four hours. We were very happy to double this, with much assistance from the tides. We were keen to get the boat back to Polruan. I had a work commitment in Bristol chairing an Exam Board, so we came alongside a pontoon at Kingswear to let me catch the steam train to Paignton and the mainline back to Bristol.

It was for all of us a great experience. For several years afterwards we reflected on the intensity and activity in the Solent and recognised the attraction of Fowey

Harbour and the RFYC to the Solent Clubs that came down on their fortnight summer cruises in company. For many of them the FHC swinging moorings, rather than a marina and the need for a water taxi or their tender was a real feature. Its only recently that the Club has had a seasonal pontoon, which encourages them to use the Club, where they are most welcome.

14. SAILING

Reading my hand script draft, I realised several failings – in explaining the 'how' I had neglected the 'why'. Probably for two reasons. If you have been doing something for over 50 years, inevitably much is obvious, also assuming readers know something about the topography and the engagement between the power of nature and boats. Some of these are specific, others generic, the latter underpinning all sailing.

The somewhat mechanical approach to tides in 'Up River', that is tables rather misses the point and the unpredictability of coastal tides. Whilst principally driven by the moon, all the secondary factors;
Wind strength and direction
    Barometric pressure
    Rainfall in the river catchment
    Topography, channels and headlands
    Tidal surge and bounce back
    Height of waves
Result in a microclimate of tide which easily adds half a metre to the mean tide and wave height can create storm damage, much more significant than the tide, as RFYC discovered a few years ago, when our refurbishment was damaged a few weeks after completion to the tune of £100,000.

Sea level is rising; the frequency with which it overtops the ferry steps and floods Fore Street in Fowey is increasing. The National Trust has decided which part of its ownership of a fifth of the coast of Devon and Cornwall cannot be defended indefinitely.

Tides are just one of the natural factors that in combination with the characteristics of the boat determine what you can do and help you decide. That engagement for the journey, particularly at dawn and dusk has for me a spiritual dimension. It may be location, for me Helford, or the course you steer brings back memories or recognition of the power of nature and human limitations in time and space.

As for boats, monthly magazines compare and contrast their features, performances and fittings, helping in the search for the right boat, which can easily become not the one you have, but the next one, perhaps work at enjoying what you have.

The contrast of two yachts of similar length is illustrated by what could be found in Viaduct Harbour in Auckland. Our ten visits to New Zealand in their summer offered the unique experience of being able to race a pair of detuned America's Cup yachts. These had been left behind by, I think, the Japanese after the 2003 competition when we first went to visit our younger daughter Hannah, the name on the stern of my Crabber 17 and a good sailor. They weighed about 20 tonnes, most of which was in the keel and came with a skipper and a mate who were joined by 24 totally novice crew on the open deck for what was a unique two hour experience. We had half an hour to learn in pairs, our role on eight grinder winches (bicycle pedals turned by hand on bollards). Then we had the opportunity to have a race out in the Hauraki Gulf with its many islands and high speed catamaran ferries. All that was left was to helm, after watching I asked the skipper some questions which he was kind enough to think were moderately intelligent, so my ten minutes on the helm were granted – thankfully they had dispensed with the spinnaker.

Americas Cup boat, Auckland

Alongside their mooring was a Round the World Racing Yacht 'Lion of New Zealand' which provided one week cruises with a minimum of eight paying crew. She was fully equipped with massive winches, accommodation for a full crew, large saloon, kitchen, workshop and best of all, a large centre cockpit. The Hauraki Gulf offers wonderful sailing with many inhabited and uninhabited islands. Our favourite is Great Barrier Island just over

Americas Cup boat racing, Auckland

60 miles out with a population of around 940 (2013) which offers 'off grid' living with solar power/generators and rain water collection.

Lion of New Zealand, cruise

Lion of New Zealand, Auckland

In discussion it emerged that business was not good, possibly because of the spartan accommodation, awful bunks – it was more comfortable to sleep in the cockpit. However, I convinced them that with four, they would not be losing money. Our once only crew had plenty of space and enjoyed powerful but controlled sailing and watersports in a setting close to that of the South Pacific. The six days cost what six hours on the America's Cup boat cost, the experience of each and contrast between the two was an illustration of the diversity, pleasure and sense of common achievement, blessed by a New Zealand summer during the English winter.

Lastly of course, people. Those chapters with single handed sailing are also inevitably a nautical pub crawl, for good reason, since they provide company, easy meals and local knowledge and of course the skipper is always right. Though there are moments when what you really need is the support that is at the Club.

The crew are as important as the boat. There are perhaps three types of crew. The regular crew are both entertaining and a source of knowledge and debate. Only a couple of times have I been thrown together with a 'once only' crew which can be daunting for all. The first many years ago for a few days cruising round New Zealand in lovely weather with just a skipper. The second in 2019 in a traditional 60 tonne trading schooner, with no winches and a lot of heave/ho. There was a crew of eight in the smallest two berth cabins and a skipper, mate and cook. We were sailing round Skye in June, 10 degrees centigrade and seven layers of clothes. in these circumstances the three essentials are a bottle of whisky to share, the ability to climb in and out of the top bunk without waking the occupant of the lower bunk and as many years as possible at boarding school.

Between the two are the passage crew. I have had two of these, two weeks legs in the passage as crew on what were two month cruises, in a very comfortable 40 foot yacht, with excellent electronics and navigation systems. The first was in the Spring of the London Olympics year, 2012 from Cornwall to the Western Isles. We called at Lundy and harbours in Wales, Isle of Man, Northern Ireland and Scotland and somewhat bizarrely in each country we met the Olympic torch and its entourage on its tour. Everyone was having a good time and we were not racing the clock.

The second was a bit more challenging and perhaps I was a bit older. To meet the schedule a 24 hour ferry from Plymouth to Santander was needed, where we were delayed for three days by a gale and on the fourth day we had the toughest beat of my life. Then no wind for a week, hundreds of miles under engine dodging fishing buoys in order to meet the schedule. This included going round Cape Finisterre, the most westerly headland in Europe, in the fog. When we got to the next port I sent my mother a postcard with a picture which described it as the Coast of Death, due to the Portuguese explorers coming home in the westerlies and the fog. Here we were against the clock which takes away the pleasure of cruising and makes you realise how tough those real sailors were.

Of course in all of nature, boats and people there is uncertainty. A weather forecast is just that; a squall comes from nowhere. The boat and its gear and electronics can surprise you, the preventer on the boom that does not stop the gybe. Discovering the characteristics of the crew of which you are a part, can sometimes be like peeling an onion. Long experience prepares you for the combination of these and there are usually more options than answers. Often, where possible the answer is to go with the flow and harness energy rather than battle with it. Though we are all vulnerable to not putting the turn on the winch quickly enough.

Well I hope you have reached the end of this passage and have not found it tough. It has taken me well over 14,000 words to explain seven – sailing is about nature, boats and people.

GLOSSARY

Beat	-	A series of tacks
Boom	-	A spar holding the sail down
Bowspit	-	A spar forward of the bow
Bumpkin	-	A spar aft of the stern
Centre plate	-	A wooden or metal plate in a central housing to give stability
Fore and Aft Mooring	-	Bow and stern secured to buoys
Foresails	-	Those ahead of the main mast
FHC	-	Fowey Harbour Commissioners
Frape	-	A perpetual rope attached to a buoy
Gaff	-	A spar raised up the mast to hold the sail
Gybe	-	The wind from astern, forcing the mainsail across
Loose footed	-	A sail without a boom
Mizzen	-	Mast on the stern of the boat
Neap tide	-	Least powerful tide
Port	-	'There is no red port LEFT in the bottle'
Reach	-	Wind on your side
Reef	-	Makes a sail smaller, roller, ties or slab
RFYC	-	Royal Fowey Yacht Club
Run	-	Wind behind you

Slack water	-	At the top or bottom of the tide
Spinnaker	-	A large foresail with a boom – difficult to manage
Spring tide	-	Most powerful tide
Starboard	-	On the right side of the boat
'Starboard'	-	A racing rule, giving right of way
Swinging mooring	-	The boat can rotate through 360 degrees
Tack	-	Sailing towards the wind
Tidal race	-	Strongest current at a headland with rough sea
Top sail	-	A sail on a spar, hoisted to the top of the mast – difficult to set